God Is Still Writing Your Story

Trusting God in the Unfinished Pages of Life

By Dr. Lende Click

Title: *God Is Still Writing Your Story*
Subtitle: *Trusting God in the Unfinished Pages of Life*
Author: Dr. Lende Click
Publisher: Lende Click Publishing

Scripture quotations are taken from the **King James Version (KJV)** unless otherwise indicated.

This book is written for inspirational and devotional purposes. It is not intended to replace professional medical, legal, financial, or mental health advice.

Printed in the United States of America.

First Edition

Dedication

This book is dedicated to *every heart*

that has ever waited in the dark,

cried in silence,

and wondered if God was still working.

To the weary heart,

the healing heart,

the heart still holding on by faith—

may these pages remind you

that your tears have been seen,

your story has not been forgotten,

and the *Author of your life*

is still writing with grace, purpose, and love.

And above all,

this book is dedicated to my *Lord and Savior, Jesus Christ*,

the faithful Author,

the healer of broken hearts,

and the One who never leaves the page.

Philippians 1:6

Being confident

of this very thing,

*that **He** who hath begun*

a good work in you

will perform it until

*the **Day** of Jesus Christ.*

Author's Note

There are seasons in life when the heart quietly asks questions it does not always know how to put into words.

Questions like:

Lord, are You still working?
Do You still see me here?
Will this chapter ever make sense?
Can anything beautiful still come from these unfinished places?

This book was written with those questions in mind.

It was written for the heart that is waiting.
For the soul that is healing.
For the person who has cried in silence and wondered if God was still near.
For the one who has tried to trust Him while walking through sorrow, delay, disappointment, or chapters they never would have chosen.

Perhaps that is why this book became so personal to me.

Because life is not made up only of joyful chapters. It also holds pages of grief, uncertainty, unanswered prayers, broken dreams, and tender beginnings that ask us to trust God again. There are seasons when faith feels strong and bright, and there are seasons when faith feels quieter— more like a trembling hand reaching for the Lord in the dark.

Yet through every kind of season, one truth remains:

God is still faithful.

He is still near in the hurting places.
He is still present in the quiet places.
He is still writing in the unfinished places.

And He is still able to bring hope, healing, and redemption to stories that feel broken or incomplete.

As I wrote these pages, my prayer was never simply to create a book of encouraging words. My prayer was that this book would become a companion for the reader walking through real life—the kind of life that does not always unfold neatly, the kind of life that sometimes leaves tears on the page.

I wanted these chapters to remind you that the story is not over just because the chapter is hard. I wanted them to speak gently to the weary heart and say:

You are not forgotten.
You are not abandoned.
You are not beyond God's healing touch.
And your story is still in His hands.

Some chapters in this book speak to waiting.
Some speak to heartbreak.
Some speak to silence, to ashes, to healing, to grace, and to the faith it takes to step into what comes next.

But all of them are held together by one simple truth:

The Author has not left the page.

If you are reading this book in a beautiful season, I pray it deepens your gratitude and trust in God.

If you are reading it in a painful season, I pray it becomes a quiet reminder that He is still with you. I pray it helps lift your eyes when the page feels heavy. I pray it gives you courage to keep going, even if the next step feels small.

And if you are reading it in a very unfinished season, I pray it reminds you that God does some of His deepest work in unfinished places.

One woman once said that the most comforting thought she could hold onto was not that she understood her story, but that God did. I think that is the comfort I hope this book leaves with every reader. Not that every question is answered, but that every page is still known, still seen, and still held by a faithful God.

Thank you for opening this book.

Thank you for bringing your heart, your questions, your hope, and even your pain to these pages. It is my prayer that as you read, you will sense the gentleness of the Lord, the steadiness of His love, and the quiet reassurance that He is still writing something beautiful in your life.

Wherever you are today—whether in joy, grief, waiting, healing, or the tender beginning of a new chapter—may you hear the whisper of God over your life:

**"I am still with you.
I am still working.
I am still writing your story."**

With love and prayer,
Dr. Lende Click

Contents

Introduction

God Is Still Writing Your Story

There was a season in one woman's life when she began to measure everything by what had not happened.

The prayer that had not yet been answered.
The healing that had not yet come.
The chapter that had not yet turned.
The questions that still had no clear explanation.

She loved God. She believed in Him. She knew His promises were true. And yet, if she was honest, there were moments when the unfinished places in her life felt louder than His faithfulness.

Maybe you understand that feeling.

Maybe you have looked at your life and seen beautiful things but also broken places. Maybe, you have carried hope in one hand and unanswered questions on the other. Maybe you have tried to trust God while walking through sorrow, delay, grief, disappointment, or confusion.

If so, this book is for you.

Life is made of many chapters.

Some are beautiful and full of joy.
Some are quiet and filled with waiting.
Some are painful and leave tears on the page.
And some are so unexpected that we hardly know how to walk through them.

There are chapters we gladly would read again, and there are chapters we wish had never happened at all. There are pages marked by hope, pages marked by heartbreak, and pages that still feel unfinished.

And when we are living inside one of the harder chapters, it can be tempting to believe that what hurts now is all there will ever be. We can begin to judge the whole story by one painful season. We can start to believe that because the page is unfinished, perhaps the Author has stepped away.

But that is not the truth.

Your story is not over.

That is the heartbeat of this book.

No matter what chapter you are in right now, God is still at work.
He is still near in the hurting places.
He is still faithful in the waiting places.
He is still healing in the broken places.
And He is still writing with love, grace, and purpose across every unfinished page of your life.

Sometimes we are tempted to judge the whole story by one painful chapter. We look at the tears, the unanswered prayers, the broken dreams, the delays, or the ashes, and we begin to believe that this is all there will ever be. But God does not write stories the way fear does.

He does not stop at heartbreak.
He does not abandon the unfinished.
He does not walk away from the pages that hurt.

He stays.

He heals.
He restores.
He redeems.
And He keeps writing.

This book was written for the heart that feels weary in the middle. For the soul that has cried in secret. For the person who is still waiting, still healing, still wondering if God is working in places that seem painfully quiet.

It was written to remind you that the unfinished parts of your life are not forgotten parts. The painful chapters are not beyond redemption. The tears have not gone unseen. The silence has not meant abandonment.

The Author has not left the page.

Throughout these chapters, we will walk through many of the places where faith is often tested most deeply: the waiting, the heartbreak, the unanswered questions, the unwanted chapters, the ashes, the quiet seasons, and the fragile beginnings that ask us to trust again. And in each one, my prayer is that you will see the same truth shining through:

God is still there.
God is still faithful.
God is still writing.

This is not a book that promises easy answers or tidy endings on every page. Life is often more tender than that. Some healing takes time. Some prayers take time. Some chapters do not fully make sense until much later.

But even in the not-yet, there is hope.

Because hope is not rooted in having all the answers. Hope is rooted in the character of God. And the God who holds your story is faithful, loving, wise, and near.

He sees the page you are on.
He sees the parts that ache.
He sees the places that feel unfinished.
And He is not intimidated by any of it.

He is still writing something beautiful.

So, as you begin this book, I invite you to bring your real heart with you.

Bring your questions.
Bring your grief.
Bring your weariness.
Bring your hope, even if it feels small.

Bring the whole unfinished story to the Lord.

And as you turn these pages, my prayer is that you will be comforted, strengthened, and gently reminded that your life is still in His hands.

The page may not yet be finished.
The chapter may still be unfolding.
But you can trust the Author.

Opening Scripture

Philippians 1:6
"Being confident of this very thing, that He who hath begun a good work in you will perform it until the Day of Jesus Christ."

Chapter 1

Your Story Is Not Over

Angela sat in her car long after the engine was turned off.

She had driven home in silence, barely remembering the road in front of her. The news she had just received kept replaying in her mind. Another disappointment. Another closed door. Another prayer that seemed to have no answer.

She had tried to be strong while she was with others. She had nodded, smiled politely, and held herself together. But now, alone in the quiet, the weight of it all settled heavily on her heart.

She looked down at her hands gripping the steering wheel and whispered the words many weary hearts have whispered before:

"Lord… what now?"

Maybe you have had a moment like that.

Perhaps it was not in a car. Perhaps it was in a hospital room, at the kitchen table after everyone had gone to bed, or in the silence of your bedroom when no one else could hear you cry. But you know what it feels like when life seems to pause in the middle of pain.

You know what it is like when the dream does not happen.

When the prayer has not yet been answered.
When the door stays closed.
When the waiting feels longer than you thought you could bear.

In moments like these, it is easy to believe a dangerous lie: that this painful chapter is the whole story.

It is easy to think, *this is it. This is how my life will always feel. This heartbreak, this confusion, this unfinished place, this must be the ending.*

But that is not the truth.

Your story is not over.

One painful chapter is not the end of the book. One season of grief does not define your whole life. One loss does not erase God's purpose. One disappointment does not cancel His promises.

And one long season of waiting does not mean God has stopped writing.

This is where many hearts grow weary. Not only because life is hard, but because the pain feels unfinished. We can often survive hard things if we know when they will end or why they are happening. But when the chapter stretches on and the answers do not come, the soul begins to ache with deeper questions.

Lord, are You still here?
Do You still see me?
Have You forgotten what You promised?

The beautiful truth of Scripture is that God is never absent from the unfinished pages.

He is present in the waiting.
He is present in the confusion.
He is present in the sorrow.
He is present in the silence.

Even when you cannot trace His hand, His hand is still there.

Many people silently judge their whole life by what is hurting right now. They look at one broken season and decide the future must also be broken. They look at what did not happen and assume nothing beautiful ever will. They see the unfinished page and think the Author has walked away.

But God does not abandon stories halfway through.

He is not intimidated by messy chapters. He is not discouraged by tears, delays, or wounded hearts. He does not step back because life feels complicated to you. In fact, some of His deepest work happens in the very places that seem most broken.

Sometimes He is strengthening faith.

Sometimes He is healing wounds you cannot yet see clearly. Sometimes He is closing one door because another has not yet opened. Sometimes He is protecting you in ways you will only understand later. And sometimes He is teaching you to trust Him, not only for the ending, but for the middle.

That does not make the chapter easy. But it does make it meaningful.

One woman once shared that after years of praying for restoration in her family, she reached a point where she no longer knew what to pray. She said she felt embarrassed by how tired she was. Ashamed that she still cried. Ashamed that she still asked God the same questions after so much time had passed.

But what touched me deeply was this: she kept going to God anyway.

That is faith.

Not polished faith.
Not loud faith.
Not easy faith.

But real faith.

Faith that returns to God with tears still in its eyes. Faith that says, "Lord, I do not understand, but I still need You." Faith that opens trembling hands and says, "I cannot carry this alone."

That kind of faith is precious to Him.

Philippians 1:6 reminds us of this truth:

"Being confident of this very thing, that He which hath begun a good work in you will perform it until the Day of Jesus Christ."

What God begins, He finishes.

He does not lose interest in your life.
He does not stop halfway through your healing.
He does not write beautiful beginnings and then leaves you alone in the middle.

If He has begun a good work in you, then He is still at work now.

That means what feels unfinished to you is not unfinished to Him.

What feels delayed is not forgotten.
What feels broken is not beyond redemption.
What feels confusing is not beyond His wisdom.
What feels painful is not beyond His healing touch.

There is a difference between a chapter being unfinished and a story being abandoned.

Your chapter may be unfinished.
But your story is not abandoned.

God still sees the whole picture when you can only see one painful page. He sees the tears you cried in secret, the prayers you whispered in the dark, the burdens you carry that no one else quite understands. He sees the chapter you are in, and He also sees the chapters still to come.

He sees where healing will rise.
He sees where peace will return.
He sees where strength will grow.
He sees where testimony will one day bloom from tears.

Even now, He is still writing.

That may be hard to believe when your heart is tired. And if you are tired, I want to say this gently: you do not have to pretend strength you do not have.

You can come to God weary.
You can come to Him confused.
You can come to Him disappointed.
You can come to Him with a heart that feels like it has more questions than answers.

He is not asking for perfection.
He is asking for trust.

And trust often begins very quietly.

Sometimes it sounds like worship.
Sometimes it sounds like surrender.
Sometimes it sounds like, "Lord, help me keep going today."

If that is all you can pray, it is enough.

God is still present in the middle of it all. He is still the God of resurrection, still the God of redemption, still the God who knows how to bring beauty from broken places. He is still writing hope into lives that feel weary and purpose into seasons that feel delayed.

So, if today you feel as though your life has stopped, hear this truth deep in your heart:

Your story is not over.

The chapter may be hard, but the Author is good.
The page may be unfinished, but His plan is still unfolding.
The road may be uncertain, but His hand is still leading.

And one day, you will look back and see that even here—in the waiting, in the pain, in the unanswered places—God was still writing something beautiful.

Scripture for This Chapter

Philippians 1:6
"Being confident of this very thing, that He which hath begun a good work in you will perform it until the Day of Jesus Christ."

Reflection

Have you been judging your whole life by one painful chapter?
What unfinished place do you need to surrender back to God today?

Prayer

Lord, thank You that my story is not over.
Even when life feels uncertain, painful, or unfinished, help me remember that You are still writing. Teach me to trust You in the chapters I do not understand. Heal the places in my heart that are weary, strengthen my faith, and remind me that You are the faithful Author of my life. I place every broken page into Your hands and trust that You are still working all things for good.
In Jesus' name, amen.

Closing Line

Do not judge your whole life by one painful chapter. God is still writing your story.

Chapter 2

When Life Does Not Make Sense

Evelyn sat at her kitchen table staring at the same verse she had read three times, yet none of the words seemed to settle in her heart.

Her Bible was open. Her coffee had gone cold. Morning light came softly through the window, but inside, everything felt heavy. Only a few weeks earlier, she had been full of hope. She had prayed, believed, and trusted that God would open the door she had waited on for so long.

Instead, the door closed.

Not gently. Not in a way, she understood. Just closed.

And now the questions were louder than the peace she had been trying to hold onto.

Why would God allow this?
Why would He lead me this far and not change the outcome?
Why does none of this make sense?

Maybe you have had a morning like that.

A moment when your heart was full of questions and heaven felt quiet. A moment, when you did everything, you knew to do—you prayed, you trusted, you tried to believe—and still the story unfolded in a way you did not understand.

There are seasons in life when nothing seems clear.

You pray, but the answer does not come.
You wait, but the door does not open.

You trust, but the road still feels uncertain.
And deep in your heart, you begin to ask, *Lord, why?*

Why did this happen?
Why did this relationship end?
Why did this prayer remain unanswered?
Why did this burden come now?
Why does the path ahead feel so hard to read?

These are not small questions. They are the questions many faithful people carry in quiet places.

Sometimes life unfolds in ways we never expected. What we hoped would happen does not happen. What we thought would stay is suddenly gone. What we believed would be simple becomes painfully complicated. And in those moments, it can feel as if the ground beneath us has shifted.

It is hard to trust when life does not make sense.

It is hard to keep believing when the answers are hidden.
It is hard to keep hoping when the path is covered in uncertainty.
It is hard to rest when the heart is full of questions.

This is one of the deepest struggles of faith, not only walking through pain, but walking through pain we cannot explain.

We often think that if we just understood the reason, we could bear the chapter more easily. If only God would tell us why. If only He would lay out the whole map. If only He would explain the silence, the delay, the detour, or the disappointment.

But faith was never meant to depend on full understanding.

Faith does not mean we always know why.
Faith does not mean every chapter will be explained right away.
Faith does not mean every prayer will be answered in the time or way we expected.

Faith means trusting the heart of God even when we cannot trace His hand.

That kind of trust does not come cheaply. It is usually formed in the very places where our understanding runs out. It is formed when life looks different than we imagined. It is formed when the soul is tired of questions and yet still chooses to stay near to God.

One woman shared that after losing something she loved deeply, she kept asking the Lord the same question over and over: *Why would You let this happen?* She said she felt guilty for asking, as if real faith should never wrestle. But the truth is, many of God's people have wrestled with questions.

David did.
Job did.
Habakkuk did.
Even Jesus, in His suffering, cried out from a place of deep anguish.

Questions do not mean your faith is dead. Sometimes they mean your heart is trying to hold onto God in the middle of what it cannot understand.

And God is not afraid of your questions.

You can bring every one of them to Him.

You can say, "Lord, I do not understand."
You can say, "Father, this hurts."
You can say, "God, I do not know what You are doing."
And even there, He will not turn away.

He does not love you less because you are confused.
He does not step back because you are weary.
He does not reject the trembling prayer of a brokenhearted soul.

Some of the holiest prayers are not polished at all. They are simple, honest, tearful prayers whispered in the middle of real life:

"Lord, I do not understand, but I still need You."
"Father, help me trust You here."
"God, hold me while I wait for clarity."

That kind of prayer is precious.

Proverbs 3:5 gives us a truth we know well, but often live only through struggle:

"Trust in the Lord with all thine heart; and lean not unto thine own understanding."

Those words are beautiful, but they are also deeply challenging.

Because we want understanding.
We want reasons.
We want timelines.
We want answers that make the pain easier to carry.

But God often leads us one step at a time.

He gives light for the next step, not always for the whole road. He gives grace for today, not always an explanation for tomorrow. And though that can feel uncomfortable, there is mercy in it. Because if we knew everything, we might trust in knowledge more than we trust in Him.

When the door closes and you do not know why—trust Him.
When the prayer is delayed and you do not know why—trust Him.
When life changes suddenly and you do not know why—trust Him.
When the chapter stays confusing longer than you hoped—trust Him.

Not because the situation feels good.
Not because the chapter is easy.
But because God is still good, even when life is hard.

That is one of the deepest lessons of the Christian life: God's goodness is not canceled by our confusion.

He is still good in the unanswered prayer.
He is still good in the closed door.
He is still good in the waiting room.
He is still good in the valley.
He is still good in the silence.

Just because you do not understand the chapter does not mean God has forgotten the story.

He knows exactly where you are.

He knows the burden you carry.
He knows the thoughts that keep you awake at night.
He knows the ache behind your smile.
He knows the weariness that comes from not understanding.

And He knows what He is doing, even when you do not.

Isaiah 55:8–9 reminds us that His thoughts are higher than ours and His ways greater than ours. What is confusing to us is never confusing to Him. What feels like a missing piece to us is already held together in His wisdom.

He is never surprised.
He is never uncertain.
He is never late.
He is never without purpose.

You may not understand today what He is doing.
You may not understand next month.
You may not even understand this chapter for a long time.

But one day, you may look back and see that God was protecting you, preparing you, strengthening you, redirecting you, or drawing you closer to Himself in ways you could not have seen then.

What feels confusing now may one day become part of your testimony.

Until then, trust Him in the not knowing.

Trust Him when the tears come.
Trust Him when the silence feels long.
Trust Him when the answers do not arrive on your schedule.
Trust Him when the story stays unfinished longer than you hoped.

The God who holds your life is not careless with your story.

He is wise.
He is loving.
He is faithful.

So, if life does not make sense right now, do not panic.

Be still.
Pray.
Breathe.
Rest your heart in God.

You do not have to understand everything to be held by Him.
You do not have to figure it all out to be led by Him.
You do not have to know the full story to trust the Author.

And one day, you may look back on this confusing chapter and realize that even here—even in the unanswered, the uncertain, and the unexplained—God was still leading you with love.

Scripture for This Chapter

Proverbs 3:5
"Trust in the Lord with all thine heart; and lean not unto thine own understanding."

Reflection

What part of your life feels confusing right now?
Can you place your unanswered questions into God's hands and trust Him,
even without full understanding?

Prayer

Lord, there are times when life does not make sense to me.
There are questions I cannot answer, burdens I do not fully understand,
and chapters that feel confusing and heavy. But today, I choose to trust
You. Help me not to lean on my own understanding, but to rest in Your
wisdom, Your love, and Your faithfulness. Calm my heart, strengthen my
faith, and remind me that even when I cannot see clearly, You are still
leading me.
In Jesus' name, amen.

Closing Line

**When life does not make sense, trust the One who sees the whole
story.**

Chapter 3

God Sees Every Tear

Late that night, after the house had finally grown quiet, Mary stood at her kitchen sink with one hand resting on the counter and the other pressed over her mouth to hold back a sob.

She had made it through the day.

She had answered messages.
She had smiled when people asked if she was doing okay.
She had taken care of what needed to be done.
She had kept moving.

But now, alone in silence, the weight of everything she had been carrying rose to the surface. The brave face was gone. The words she held in all day would not come. Only tears came.

Tears for what she had lost.
Tears for what had not changed.
Tears for the ache she did not know how to explain.

Maybe you have known a moment like that.

A moment when you held yourself together for everyone else, only to fall apart when no one was looking. A moment when the tears came, not because you were weak, but because your heart had been carrying too much for too long.

There are tears that no one else sees.

Tears cried behind closed doors.
Tears that fall in the silence of the night.

Tears hidden behind a smile.
Tears that come from places words cannot fully reach.

Some tears come from heartbreak.
Some come from disappointment.
Some come from grief, loneliness, betrayal, or fear.
And some come simply because the soul is tired.

One of the hardest parts of pain is how invisible it can feel.

People may see your face but not your sorrow.
They may hear your voice but not the ache beneath it.
They may notice you are quieter than usual, but they do not know the
prayers you have whispered through tears.

But God knows.

He sees every tear that falls from your eyes.
He sees the ones that come quickly and the ones you fight to hold back.
He sees the tears of deep grief and the tears of quiet exhaustion.
He sees the tears no one else ever knew were there.

Not one tear is wasted in His sight.

Psalm 56:8 gives us one of the tenderest pictures in all of Scripture:

**"Thou tellest my wanderings: put thou my tears into Thy bottle: are
they not in Thy book?"**

What a beautiful truth.

God does not overlook your tears.
He does not ignore your sorrow.
He does not hurry past your pain as if it does not matter.

He gathers every tear.

The tears you cried after the phone call that changed everything.
The tears you cried when the prayer was not answered the way you hoped.
The tears you cried because someone hurt you deeply.
The tears you cried because your heart felt tired, alone, and worn thin.

God saw them all.

That means your pain has never been hidden from Him.
Your sorrow has never gone unnoticed.
Your heartbreak has never been dismissed.

Even when others did not understand, God understood.
Even when others did not notice, God noticed.
Even when others walked away, God remained.

There is deep comfort in knowing that the Lord does not only see our victories—He also sees our tears.

He sees the woman who is strong for everyone else but feels weak inside. He sees the mother who cries in the bathroom so her children will not hear. He sees the widow who reaches for the other side of the bed and feels the emptiness all over again. He sees the one who keeps showing up, keeps functioning, keeps trying, even while carrying private sorrow.

He sees more than the tear itself.

He sees what caused it.
He sees the memory behind it.
He sees the wound beneath it.
He sees the burden attached to it.

And He cares.

Sometimes the enemy whispers cruel things in our grief. He tells us no one cares. He tells us we should be stronger by now. He tells us tears are weakness. But that is not the voice of God.

Your tears are not proof that you are weak.
Sometimes they are proof that you have been strong for too long.

There is no shame in tears.

Jesus Himself wept.

The Savior who calmed storms also stood at a grave and cried. The Son of God was not untouched by sorrow. He knows what grief feels like. He knows what it means to love deeply and to ache deeply.

So, when you cry, you are not crying before a distant God who does not understand. You are crying before a Savior who knows sorrow from the inside and who meets hurting hearts with compassion.

And because He knows, He, is able to comfort.

One woman once shared that after a painful season in her family, she stopped trying to pray long prayers. She said some nights all she could manage was, "Lord, You see me." That was all she had. No polished words. No strength left to explain the whole story.

But maybe that is one of the most powerful prayers a hurting heart can pray:

Lord, You see me.

You see this pain.
You see this grief.
You see this exhaustion.
You see the tears I hide from everyone else.

And the beautiful answer of Scripture is yes—He does.

Second Corinthians calls Him the God of all comfort. Not some comfort. Not distant comfort. Not cold advice from afar. Real comfort. Near comfort. Personal comfort.

Sometimes His comfort comes through His Word.
Sometimes it comes in prayer.
Sometimes it comes through a quiet peace that settles over the heart.
Sometimes it comes through a friend, a kind word, or simply the strength to make it through another day.

However it comes, His comfort is real.

Psalm 34:18 says:

"The Lord is nigh unto them that are of a broken heart; and saveth such as be of a contrite spirit."

Near.

That word matters.

When your heart is broken, God is near.
When your tears fall, God is near.
When the room feels quiet and the burden feels lonely, God is near.
When you do not have words for what hurts, God is near.

You may not always feel Him, but He has not left you.
You may not always understand what He is doing, but He has not forgotten you.
You may not always know how healing will come, but He is still the God who heals.

Sometimes tears are part of healing.

We often want to stop crying quickly. We want the pain to go away fast. We want the heart to feel whole again immediately. But healing is not always instant. Sometimes God heals gently, slowly, and deeply—layer by layer, prayer by prayer, tear by tear.

And that does not mean He is absent.

It means He is working beneath the surface.

He is healing, places no one else can reach.
He is touching memories no one else can mend.
He is strengthening parts of your soul that have grown tired under the weight of pain.

So do not despise your tears.

They are not wasted.
They are not forgotten.
They are not unseen.

God sees everyone.

And one day, the same God who held your tears will wipe them away.

Revelation 21:4 gives us this precious hope:

"And God shall wipe away all tears from their eyes; and there shall be no more death, neither sorrow, nor crying, neither shall there be any more pain: for the former things are passed away."

What a promise.

The tears of this life are not forever.
The sorrow of this world is not forever.
The brokenness of this chapter is not forever.

A day is coming when pain will end and tears will cease. But until that day, you are held by the God who sees, the God who comforts, and the God who stays near.

So, if tears have been your language lately, let this truth settle deeply into your heart:

God sees every tear.
He sees the ones you cried yesterday.
He sees the ones you cry today.

He sees the ones you have not yet cried but already feel gathering in your chest.

He sees, and He cares.

You do not have to hide your sorrow from Him.
You do not have to pretend to be stronger than you feel.
You do not have to carry silent grief by yourself.

Bring every tear to the Lord.

Bring Him the heartbreak.
Bring Him the disappointment.
Bring Him the weariness.
Bring Him the ache you cannot fully explain.

He is gentle with hurting hearts.
He is faithful with fragile souls.
And He will not waste a single tear.

Scripture for This Chapter

Psalm 56:8
"Thou tellest my wanderings: put thou my tears into thy bottle: are they not in thy book?"

Reflection

What tears have you been carrying in silence?
Can you bring your sorrow honestly to God and trust that He sees and cares deeply for every pain in your heart?

Prayer

Lord, thank You that You see every tear I cry.
Thank You that my pain is not hidden from You and my sorrow is not forgotten. When my heart feels heavy, broken, or weary, remind me that You are near. Comfort me with Your presence, heal the places in me that are hurting, and help me trust that not one tear is wasted in Your hands. Hold me close in every sorrow and strengthen me with Your peace.
In Jesus' name, amen.

Closing Line

Not one tear falls without God seeing it, holding it, and caring for the heart that cried it.

Chapter 4

Trusting God in the Middle

Danielle had been praying for months, maybe longer, for the same thing.

At first, she prayed with bright hope. She believed the answer would come quickly. She imagined the breakthrough, the relief, the day she would look back and thank God for bringing her through.

But the answer did not come quickly.

Weeks turned into months. Months stretched longer than she expected. And now she found herself in a place that felt harder than in the beginning.

The middle.

Not at the start, where hope had first risen strong.
Not at the end, where everything would finally make sense.
But in the long in-between place, where she was still waiting, still praying, still trying to trust God one day at a time.

Maybe you know that place.

It is the place between the prayer and the answer.
The place between the promise and the fulfillment.
The place between the hurt and the healing.
The place where you are still hoping, still believing, and still asking God for strength to keep going.

The middle can be a very hard place to live.

The beginning often carries hope. There is something fresh about the start of a prayer, a dream, or a season of believing God. And the ending, one day, may reveal His beautiful purpose. But the middle is different. The middle feels unfinished. It feels uncertain. It feels heavy.

It is where the heart whispers,
Lord, how much longer?

It is where tears and faith often meet.
It is where you keep walking, even when the road is unclear.
It is where you keep showing up to pray, even when you do not yet see movement.

Many people know how to praise God at the beginning of a blessing. Many know how to thank Him after the breakthrough has come. But trusting Him in the middle—when nothing is finished yet, when the answer has not come, when the story still feels unresolved, that is where deep faith is often formed.

The middle is where trust becomes real.

It is not always loud faith.
It is not always confident faith.
Sometimes it is quiet, trembling faith.

Faith that wakes up and prays again.
Faith that says, *"Lord, I still trust You,"* even with unanswered questions.
Faith that keeps walking when the heart feels tired.

That kind of faith is precious.

It is difficult to trust God when you are still in pain.
It is difficult to trust Him when the door is still closed.
It is difficult to trust Him when the prayer feels delayed.
It is difficult to trust Him when you thought something would have changed by now.

The middle can wear on the soul.

You may wonder if God hears you.
You may wonder if He remembers His promise.
You may wonder if the breakthrough will ever come.
You may wonder if you are walking in the right direction at all.

But the middle does not mean God has left the story.

The middle is not proof of His absence.
It is not proof that your prayers were ignored.
It is not proof that your waiting is wasted.
It is not proof that the promise has died.

Sometimes the middle is the very place where God is doing His deepest work.

This is something we do not always see while we are living in it. In the middle, God often works beneath the surface. He stretches faith. He softens hearts. He teaches surrenders. He reveals how deeply we need Him. He teaches us to walk by faith, not by sight.

We often want God to take us quickly from prayer to promise, from sorrow to joy, from need to provision. But sometimes He keeps us in the middle longer than we expected—not to harm us, but to shape us.

There is purpose in the middle.

There is growth in the middle.
There is surrender in the middle.
There is strengthening in the middle.
There is holy preparation in the middle.

Even when you cannot yet see the fruit, God is still working.

A seed hidden in the ground may look forgotten, but it is not dead. Something is happening where human eyes cannot yet see it. In the same way, the season you are in may feel buried, quiet, and slow, but God is not absent from it. He is still at work in places your eyes cannot yet reach.

What feels still to you is not still to God.
What feels slow to you is not forgotten by God.
What feels unfinished to you is still in His hands.

Isaiah 40:31 gives such comfort in seasons like this:

"But they that wait upon the Lord shall renew their strength; they shall mount up with wings as eagles; they shall run, and not be weary; and they shall walk, and not faint."

That verse reminds us that waiting with God is not empty. It is a place where strength is renewed.

Not always all at once.
Not always in dramatic ways.
But little by little, God gives grace for the middle.

He gives strength for today.
He gives peace for today.
He gives mercy for today.
He gives daily bread for the soul.

Sometimes we want tomorrow's answers, but God gives today's grace.

And today's grace is enough.

One woman once said that what surprised her most in a long waiting season was not that God gave her all the answers, but that He kept giving her enough strength for one more day. One more prayer. One more surrender. One more step.

That is how many of us make it through the middle.

Not by having the whole map.
Not by feeling strong every moment.
Not by knowing exactly how the chapter will turn out.

But by receiving grace for today.

When you are in the middle, it is easy to focus on what has not happened yet. It is easy to feel discouraged by how far there still is to go. But faith learns to trust God not only for the ending, but also for the journey.

Trust Him in the waiting.
Trust Him in the unanswered prayer.
Trust Him in the delay.
Trust Him in the unclear places.
Trust Him in the chapter that still has blank pages.

You may not see the full picture, but you are still held by the One who does.

Sometimes God keeps us in the middle so that we will know Him more deeply than we would have known Him in an easier season. In the middle, prayer becomes more real. Dependence becomes more honest. Worship becomes more costly and more precious. And trust becomes less about feelings and more about surrender.

The middle teaches us that God is good before the answer comes.
He is faithful before the breakthrough comes.
He is near before the healing is complete.
He is worthy before the promise is fulfilled.

That kind of faith is beautiful in His sight.

If you feel weary in the middle, do not be ashamed of your weakness. Bring it to God. Tell Him you are tired. Tell Him the waiting feels long. Tell Him your heart needs strength. He already knows, and He is gentle with weary souls.

He is not asking you to carry tomorrow all at once.
He is asking you to trust Him today.

Today's trust.
Today's prayer.
Today's surrender.
Today's faith.

That is how you walk through the middle.

Psalm 37:23–24 gives us another beautiful picture:

"The steps of a good man are ordered by the Lord, and He delighteth in his way. Though he fall, he shall not be utterly cast down; for the Lord upholdeth him with His hand."

What a comfort to know that even if you feel unsteady, you are still upheld.

You may feel unsteady, but you are upheld.
You may feel tired, but you are sustained.
You may feel uncertain, but you are still being led.

The middle is not easy, but it is not godless.

God is in the middle.
He is in the waiting.
He is in the silence.
He is in the unanswered place.
He is in the slow work of becoming, healing, trusting, and growing.

And because He is there, the middle is not wasted.

One day, you may look back and realize that the middle was where your faith deepened, where your heart softened, where your dependence on God became more real, and where His presence became more precious than the answer you were waiting for.

So do not despise the middle.

Do not rush past it in your heart.
Do not call it empty just because it is unfinished.
Do not think God is absent just because the story is still unfolding.

The middle matters.

It is where trust learns to stand.
It is where faith learns to breathe.
It is where the soul learns that God is enough, even here.

So, if you are in the middle today, take courage.

God is still with you.
God is still leading you.
God is still strengthening you.
God is still writing.

And He will be faithful in every page you have not yet read.

Scripture for This Chapter

Isaiah 40:31
"But they that wait upon the Lord shall renew their strength; they shall mount up with wings as eagles; they shall run, and not be weary; and they shall walk, and not faint."

Reflection

What "middle place" are you walking through right now?
How can you choose to trust God today, even before you see the outcome?

Prayer

Lord, sometimes the middle feels long and hard.
I grow tired in the waiting, and my heart longs for answers, healing, and clarity. But today I choose to trust You in the middle. Strengthen me where I feel weak, renew me where I feel weary, and remind me that You are still with me in every unfinished place. Help me walk by faith, one day

at a time, and rest in Your presence while You continue to write my story. In Jesus' name, amen.

33

Closing Line

The middle may be unfinished, but it is never outside the hands of God.

Chapter 5

The Purpose in the Waiting

Teresa folded the same prayer list and slipped it back into her Bible.

The paper was soft at the creases from being opened so many times. Some of the prayers on it were old now. She had written them with hope, with expectation, with faith that surely the answer would come soon. But days had become months, and months had stretched longer than she ever thought they would.

She was still waiting.

Waiting for healing.
Waiting for change.
Waiting for the door to open.
Waiting for God to move in the places that still felt painfully still.

And as she sat there in the quiet, one question rose again in her heart:

Lord, why is this taking so long?

Maybe you have known that question too.

Maybe you have prayed with all your heart and then watched time pass without the answer you hoped for. Maybe you have stood in the tension between faith and delay, trying to trust God while part of you feels weary from the waiting.

Waiting can be one of the hardest parts of life.

It is not easy to wait when your heart is hoping.
It is not easy to wait when you have prayed for so long.

It is not easy to wait when you are ready for answers, ready for healing, ready for change, and ready for the next chapter to begin.

Waiting can feel quiet.
It can feel slow.
It can feel lonely.
And sometimes it can even feel discouraging.

You may wonder if your prayers are still before Him.
You may wonder if the promise is still coming.
You may wonder if anything is happening at all.

But just because you do not see movement does not mean God is not working.

That is one of the deepest truths of the Christian life: heaven is not silent because heaven is absent. God is often doing unseen work long before we see visible change. What looks still to us may be full of holy preparation in His hands.

Waiting is never wasted when it is placed in God's hands.

To us, waiting often feels like delay.
But to God, waiting is often preparation.

What feels slow to you may be holy timing.
What feels hidden to you may be deep work.
What feels still to you may be God moving in places you cannot yet see.

We naturally want quick answers. We want the prayer answered now. We want the healing now. We want the open door now. We want the breakthrough now. We want the dream to come alive now.

But God does not work by human impatience.

He works, by perfect wisdom.

Ecclesiastes 3:11 says:

"He hath made every thing beautiful in his time."

Not always in our time.
Not always in our preferred way.
But in His time.

That can be difficult for the heart to accept. Because waiting stretches us in ways comfort never does. It stretches faith. It stretches patience. It stretches surrender. It stretches our desire to control what only God can carry.

And yet, in that stretching, God is doing something valuable.

Waiting is not just about what you are hoping for.
It is also about what God is doing in you while you wait.

Sometimes we become so focused on the thing we are waiting for that we miss the quiet work God is doing inside our hearts. Yet often, the waiting season is where some of the deepest spiritual growth takes place.

In waiting, God teaches us to trust Him more deeply.
In waiting, He teaches us to pray more honestly.
In waiting, He teaches us to release control.
In waiting, He teaches us to rest in His goodness, not just in His gifts.

One woman once said that during a long season of waiting, she thought the main story was the thing she was praying for. But later she realized the deeper story was what God had been shaping in her while she waited. He was teaching her endurance. He was softening places of fear. He was drawing her closer to Himself.

That is often how God works.

Waiting has a way of revealing what is in the heart.

It can reveal fear.
It can reveal impatience.
It can reveal weariness.
It can reveal how much we long to understand everything.

But it can also become a sacred place where faith is refined.

Romans 5:3–4 reminds us, that tribulation worketh patience; and patience, experience; and experience, hope. God can use difficult seasons to produce something lasting in us.

Patience is not weakness.
Patience is strength that has learned to rest in God.

There is a quiet strength in the person who keeps praying while waiting.
There is a quiet beauty in the person who keeps trusting while waiting.
There is a quiet power in the heart that says,
"Lord, I do not understand Your timing, but I still believe You are good."

That kind of waiting honors God.

It is not passive.
It is not empty.
It is not doing, nothing.

Biblical waiting is active trust.

It is praying while waiting.
It is obeying while waiting.
It is worshiping while waiting.
It is believing while waiting.
It is choosing hope, while the answer is still on the way.

Isaiah 64:4 tells us that God acts on behalf of those who wait for Him. What a comfort. That means heaven is not ignoring you in your waiting season. God is not forgetting you. He is not losing your prayers. He is not overlooking your tears.

He is working.

Even if you cannot see it yet.
Even if the answer feels delayed.
Even if the chapter still looks unfinished.

Sometimes God makes us wait because He is protecting us.

A door may remain closed because the timing is not right.
A prayer may seem delayed because He is preparing something better.
A season may last longer because He is developing strength in you that you will need for what comes next.

What feels like delay may actually be mercy.

What feels like silence may actually be wisdom.
What feels like a closed chapter may actually be divine protection.

God sees what you do not see.

He sees the future.
He sees the people, places, and details you cannot yet know.
He sees what must be moved, healed, arranged, or prepared before the next page is ready to turn.

That is why you can trust Him in the waiting.

He is not careless with your life.
He is not slow because He forgot you.
He is not silent because He stopped caring.

He is wise, loving, and intentional.

Psalm 27:14 says:

"Wait on the Lord: be of good courage, and He shall strengthen thine heart: wait, I say, on the Lord."

I love that verse because it does not pretend waiting is easy. It calls for courage.

Waiting takes courage when the heart is tired.
Waiting takes courage when hope has been stretched.
Waiting takes courage when you have cried and prayed and wondered how much longer.

But God promises strength for the waiting heart.

He does not leave you alone in it.
He strengthens your heart while you wait.

That means the waiting season is not only about the answer you want. It is also about the heart God is strengthening.

Perhaps you are waiting for healing.
Perhaps you are waiting for restoration.
Perhaps you are waiting for open doors, provision, clarity, or peace.

Whatever you are waiting for, remember this:

The God who calls you to wait is the same God who will sustain you while you wait.

He will give grace for the slow days.
He will give peace for the uncertain days.
He will give comfort for the tearful days.
He will give strength for the days when you feel like giving up.

And when the time is right, He knows how to turn the page.

Until then, do not despise the waiting.

Do not call it empty just because it is quiet.
Do not call it pointless just because it is slow.
Do not call it forgotten just because the answer has not yet arrived.

There is purpose, in the waiting.

There is preparation in the waiting.
There is refining in the waiting.
There is intimacy with God in the waiting.
There is deepening faith in the waiting.

Sometimes the waiting season becomes the very place where you learn that Jesus is enough before the answer comes. And that lesson is precious beyond words.

One day, you may look back and realize that the waiting was not just a gap in your story. It was a holy chapter where God was shaping your heart, strengthening your faith, and preparing the next page with perfect wisdom.

So, if you are waiting today, do not lose heart.

Keep praying.
Keep trusting.
Keep obeying.
Keep surrendering.
Keep placing your hope in the Lord.

Because the waiting is not wasted.

God is still working.
God is still preparing.
God is still strengthening.
God is still writing your story.

And His timing will never fail.

Scripture for This Chapter

Psalm 27:14
"Wait on the Lord: be of good courage, and he shall strengthen thine heart: wait, I say, on the Lord."

Reflection

What are you waiting on God for right now?
How might God be strengthening, teaching, or preparing you in this season of waiting?

Prayer

Lord, waiting is not always easy for me.
Sometimes my heart grows tired, and I want answers faster than they come. But help me trust Your timing. Strengthen me in the waiting, teach me what You want me to learn, and help me believe that this season is not wasted. Remind me that You are still working, even when I cannot see it. Give me courage, peace, and patience as I place every unanswered prayer into Your faithful hands.
In Jesus' name, amen.

Closing Line

What feels like delay to you may be God's loving preparation for something beautiful in His time.

Chapter 6

When a Chapter Breaks Your Heart

Lorraine sat on the edge of her bed, still holding the phone long after the call had ended.

The room was quiet, but her heart was not.

What she had just heard had settled into her like a weight. She tried to breathe normally. She tried to steady herself. But the pain of it spread through her chest too quickly to ignore. There are moments in life when disappointment hurts. And then there are moments when something breaks open inside you.

This was one of those moments.

Maybe you have known one too.

Maybe it came through a phone call.
Maybe it came through words someone said.
Maybe it came through a door closing, a dream falling apart, or a loss you never saw coming.

Some chapters of life break the heart in ways words can barely explain.

They are the chapters you never wanted.
The ones you never would have chosen.
The ones filled with loss, disappointment, betrayal, grief, silence, or pain so deeply it changes something inside you.

There are seasons when the heart feels bruised.

There are moments when life does not only hurt—it breaks you open. And in those chapters, even ordinary things can feel heavy. Getting up feels heavy. Smiling feels heavy. Talking feels heavy. Sometimes even breathing feels heavy.

A broken heart carries many questions.

Why did this happen?
Why did they leave?
Why did this door close?
Why did the prayer go unanswered?
Why did the pain come so suddenly, or stay so long?

Sometimes there are no quick answers.

And that can be part of what makes heartbreak so painful. It is not only the hurt itself. It is the confusion that often comes with it. It is the way heartbreak shakes what once felt steady. It is the way sorrow can make the world feel unfamiliar.

Sometimes a chapter breaks your heart not because you lack faith, but because you are human and living in a world where sorrow is real. Even those who love God deeply walk through painful chapters. Even those who pray, trust, and believe still experience grief, disappointment, betrayal, and loss.

A broken heart is not proof that God has left you.

It is proof that you have loved, hoped, trusted, and felt deeply.

And God is not unmoved by the things that have broken you.

Psalm 34:18 says:

"The Lord is nigh unto them that are of a broken heart; and saveth such as be of a contrite spirit."

What a tender promise.

Not far.
Not distant.
Not watching from afar.

Near.

When your heart is broken, God comes near.

He does not wait for you to have everything together.
He does not wait for you to stop crying.
He does not wait for you to explain your pain perfectly.

He draws near to the brokenhearted.

That means in the chapter that shattered you, God did not step away. In the moment that wounded you, He was still present. In the sorrow you did not know how to carry, He was still holding you—even if you could not feel it then.

Heartbreak comes in many forms.

Sometimes it comes through loss.

The loss of a person.
The loss of a dream.
The loss of a relationship.
The loss of the future you thought you would have.

Grief has a way of touching every part of the soul. It can make ordinary days feel heavy. It can make memories ache. It can make the future feel unfamiliar. When the heart is grieving, it is not weak. It is wounded.

Sometimes heartbreak comes through betrayal.

There is a particular kind of pain when the wound comes from someone you trusted. When loyalty is broken, when words cut deeply, when someone you loved handles your heart carelessly, the pain can feel sharp and disorienting.

Sometimes heartbreak comes through disappointment.

The prayer you carried for years.
The answer you thought would come.
The opportunity you believed would open.
The story you hoped would unfold differently.

Disappointment hurts because it lives so close to hope.

And when hope hurts, the heart can grow tired.

One woman once shared that after a painful loss, what troubled her most
was not only the sorrow itself, but how changed she felt by it. She said, "I
don't know how to be the person I was before." That is often how
heartbreak feels. It does not only wound the moment. It can reshape how
everything feels for a while.

But even when a chapter breaks your heart, God is still able to hold every
broken piece.

He is not afraid of shattered places.
He is not overwhelmed by your sorrow.
He is not discouraged by the depth of your pain.

The same God who formed your heart knows how to care for it when it
breaks.

Sometimes we try to hide heartbreak from God. We think we must stay
strong, say the right words, and appear steady. But God is not asking you
to pretend. He invites honesty.

You can tell Him,
"Lord, this chapter hurts."
You can tell Him,
"Father, I do not know how to carry this."
You can tell Him,
"God, my heart is broken."

And He will not turn away.

Psalm 147:3 says:

"He healeth the broken in heart, and bindeth up their wounds."

That verse is full of mercy.

It tells us that broken hearts can be healed.
It tells us that wounds can be bound up.
It tells us that the God who sees the pain is also the God who tends to it.

Healing does not always happen in one moment. Sometimes God heals gently and slowly. Sometimes He binds the wound little by little, with grace for each day. Sometimes the heart still aches while healing is already quietly beginning beneath the surface.

But healing is still possible.

Even for the heart that feels deeply wounded.
Even for the chapter that left scars.
Even for the soul that feels tired from carrying so much pain.

God knows how to bring healing without rushing your heart.
He knows how to be gentle with your grief.
He knows how to strengthen what sorrow has weakened.

When a chapter breaks your heart, it may feel like the story has been ruined. It may feel like something beautiful has been lost forever. But a painful chapter does not cancel God's ability to redeem.

He still writes hope after heartbreak.
He still writes healing after hurt.
He still writes peace after pain.
He still writes purpose after loss.

The broken chapter may one day become part of your testimony—not because the pain was good, but because God is good enough to bring something holy from what hurt you.

Romans 8:28 reminds us that God works all things together for good to them that love Him. That does not mean every painful thing is good. It means God is able to take even painful things and weave them into a greater story of grace.

Only God can do that.

Only God can sit with you in sorrow and still whisper hope.
Only God can begin restoration in the same place where something fell apart.
Only God can meet a broken heart with such tenderness.

If you are walking through a chapter that has broken your heart, be gentle with yourself.

Healing hearts often need time.
Grieving hearts often need rest.
Wounded hearts often need truth, prayer, and the steady presence of God.

Do not be ashamed that this chapter affected you deeply.
Do not believe the lie that strong people never cry.
Do not believe that faith means never feeling pain.

Faith is not the absence of heartbreak.

Faith is choosing to bring your heartbreak to God.

It is letting Him into the wound.
It is letting Him sit with you in the sorrow.
It is trusting that even if this chapter broke your heart, it did not break His power to heal, restore, and redeem.

One day, you may look back and realize that the chapter which broke your heart also drove you closer to the heart of God. You may see that in the place of deepest pain; He met you with deepest mercy. You may discover that the chapter you feared would destroy you became the place where His comfort held you most closely.

So do not lose hope.

Your broken heart is not beyond God's touch.
Your wounded soul is not beyond His healing.
Your painful chapter is not beyond His redemption.

He is near to you now.
He is gentle with you now.
He is still carrying you now.

And though the chapter may have broken your heart, it has not ended your story.

God still knows how to write beauty after heartbreak.

Scripture for This Chapter

Psalm 147:3
"He healeth the broken in heart, and bindeth up their wounds."

Reflection

What chapter of your life has broken your heart most deeply?
Can you bring that broken place honestly to God and trust Him to begin healing, even if it takes time?

Prayer

Lord, You know every chapter that has broken my heart.
You know the loss, the sorrow, the disappointment, and the pain I have
carried. Thank You for being near to the brokenhearted and for not turning
away from my tears. Please heal the places in me that are wounded, bind
up what has been broken, and gently restore my heart with Your love and
peace. Help me trust that even this painful chapter is not beyond Your
redeeming power.
In Jesus' name, amen.

Closing Line

**A chapter may break your heart, but it can never remove you from
the healing hands of God.**

Chapter 7

God Can Heal What Was Broken

Naomi ran her fingers along the edge of an old photograph before setting it back inside the drawer.

There were some memories she could look at without falling apart now, and for that she was thankful. But there were other places in her heart that still felt tender. Still unfinished. Still bruised in ways no one else could fully see.

What had broken in her life, had not all broken at once.

Some things had broken quietly.

Trust had broken.
Peace had broken.
Hope had broken, in places she once thought were strong.
And something inside her heart had cracked under the weight of carrying too much for too long.

Maybe you understand that kind of brokenness.

Not always dramatic.
Not always visible.
But real.

Sometimes brokenness comes with one terrible moment. Sometimes it comes slowly, through disappointment, grief, betrayal, fear, or long seasons of pain. Sometimes it comes through words that wounded deeply. Sometimes it comes through loss that changed you. Sometimes it comes from simply surviving too much for too long without rest for the soul.

And when something has been broken, it is easy to wonder if it will ever truly be whole again.

Will this pain ever heal?
Will this heart ever feel peace again?
Will this wounded place always ache?
Will I always carry the weight of this chapter?

These are tender questions. And they often rise from very real pain.

But here is the hope we must hold onto:

God can heal what was broken.

Not from a distance.
Not with hurried hands.
Not with cold indifference.

But deeply, lovingly, and faithfully in His perfect way.

God is not helpless in the face of brokenness.
He is not limited by the damage.
He is not discouraged by how deep the wound goes.

The places that seem shattered to you are not beyond His power to restore.

Jeremiah 30:17a says:

"For I will restore health unto thee, and I will heal thee of thy wounds, saith the Lord."

What a beautiful promise.

The God who made the heart knows how to heal the heart.
The God who formed your soul knows how to restore your soul.
The God who sees every hidden wound knows how to touch the places no one else can reach.

Sometimes we live with pain so long that we begin to assume it will always stay the same. We grow used to the ache. We learn how to function around it. We smile when we need to smile, keep moving when we need to keep moving, and quietly carry broken places we no longer know how to name.

But brokenness is not a final sentence in the hands of the Lord.

He is still the God who restores.
Still the God who mends.
Still the God who breathes life into weary places.
Still the God who makes beauty from ashes.

One woman once shared that after years of carrying hurt, she had stopped asking God for healing in that area of her life. Not because she no longer believed He could heal, but because she had gotten used to living around the wound. She had built emotional walls around it. She had learned how to survive with it. But one day, in prayer, she sensed the Lord gently asking her a question: ***Do you want Me to heal what you have learned to hide?***

That is such a tender question.

Because many of us want healing, but we are also afraid of it. Healing asks us to open the places we have protected. It asks us to bring the wound into the light. It asks us to trust God with the very places that once felt too painful to touch.

And yet, that is where grace begins to move.

Healing is one of God's mercies.

Sometimes He heals in a moment.
Sometimes He heals over time.
Sometimes He heals through tears, truth, prayer, surrender, and His steady presence day after day.

But however He chooses to heal, He is faithful.

Healing does not always mean the memory disappears.
It does not always mean the scar is gone.
It does not always mean the chapter never mattered.

Sometimes healing means the wound no longer controls you.
Sometimes healing means peace returns where torment once lived.
Sometimes healing means your heart can breathe again.
Sometimes healing means you can remember without being crushed by what happened.

That is real healing.

God's healing reaches deeper than appearances. He does not only smooth the surface. He touches the root of pain. He sees what lies underneath the anger, the fear, the exhaustion, the silence, and the grief. He knows where the wound began, and He knows how to minister to it with perfect wisdom.

Psalm 147:3 says:

"He healeth the broken in heart, and bindeth up their wounds."

He heals.
He binds up.
He tends.
He cares.

This is not the picture of a distant God.
This is the picture of a tender Father.

He does not shame you for what broke.
He does not scold you for still hurting.
He does not rush you when healing feels slow.

He binds up wounds.

That means He handles broken places with care.
He knows wounded hearts often need gentleness.

He knows recovery takes grace.
He knows some wounds cannot be treated carelessly.

And He is never careless with your heart.

Sometimes brokenness leaves us afraid to hope again.

We fear being hurt again.
We fear trusting again.
We fear opening our hearts to God's healing because we do not want to feel vulnerable in the places that once caused so much pain.

But healing begins when we let God into the broken place.

Not hiding it.
Not pretending it does not hurt.
Not covering it with busyness, strength, or silence.

But opening the wound to the One who can truly heal it.

That can be a sacred and vulnerable surrender.

It may sound like this:

"Lord, this is the place that still hurts."
"Father, this is the wound I have carried."
"God, this is the broken place I need You to heal."

And when you bring it to Him, He does not turn away.

Jesus was never afraid of broken people.

He drew near to them.
He touched lepers.
He comforted the grieving.
He lifted the fallen.
He restored the hurting.

And He still does.

The same Jesus who healed bodies also heals hearts.
The same Savior who calmed storms also calms troubled souls.
The same Lord who raised the dead can breathe hope into places that feel
lifeless inside you.

Nothing broken is too broken for Him.

Not the heart that has been betrayed.
Not the soul that has been weary for years.
Not the life that feels torn apart.
Not the dream that fell apart in your hands.

God is able.

He may not always heal in the timeline you prefer.
He may not always restore in the exact form you expected.
But He knows how to bring healing that is real, deep, and lasting.

Sometimes what God restores does not look exactly like what was lost.
Sometimes it looks wiser, stronger, deeper, and more anchored in Him.
Sometimes He does not simply take you back to who you were before the
pain. Sometimes He brings you forward into greater wholeness than you
knew before.

That is the mercy of God.

Joel 2:25 gives us another tender promise:

"And I will restore to you the years that the locust hath eaten..."

Only God can restore years.
Only God can reach into wasted seasons and bring redemption.
Only God can take what seemed lost and breathe purpose into it again.

If the enemy has convinced you that the broken places in your life will
always define you, reject that lie.

Your wound is not your identity.
Your broken chapter is not your final name.
Your pain is not the end of your story.

God's healing is greater than what hurt you.

That does not mean the journey is always easy. Healing often asks for honesty. It asks for surrender. It asks for letting God uncover what has been hidden and speak truth where lies have lived. It asks for trusting Him again, even in the places that once felt unsafe.

But He will walk with you through every part of it.

He does not stand only at the finish line.
He walks beside you in the process.
He gives daily grace.
He gives daily comfort.
He gives daily strength.

And little by little, what was once broken begins to breathe again.

The heart begins to soften.
Peace begins to return.
Hope begins to rise.
Joy begins to visit again.
And the soul begins to believe that healing is not just possible—it is already beginning.

So, if you are carrying broken places today, do not give up.

Bring them to Jesus.
Bring Him the shattered trust.
Bring Him the broken dream.
Bring Him the wounded memory.
Bring Him the pain you still do not know how to explain.

He can heal what was broken.

He can restore what was wounded.
He can strengthen what grew weak.
He can revive what felt lifeless.
He can bring beauty where sorrow once lived.

And one day, you may look back and see that the place you thought would always remain broken became the very place where God's healing mercy shone the brightest.

Scripture for This Chapter

Jeremiah 30:17
"For I will restore health unto thee, and I will heal thee of thy wounds, saith the Lord."

Reflection

What broken place in your heart still needs God's healing touch?
Are you willing to open that wound to Him and trust that He can restore what feels damaged or lost?

Prayer

Lord, You see every broken place in me.
You know the wounds I carry, the pain I still remember, and the places in my heart that need Your healing. Thank You that nothing is too broken for You. Please restore what has been wounded, heal what has been shattered, and breathe new hope into every place that has grown weary. Help me trust Your gentle healing process and believe that You are still able to make me whole.
In Jesus' name, amen.

Closing Line

What was broken in your life is not beyond the restoring hands of God.

Chapter 8

The Chapters You Did Not Choose

Rebecca stood in the doorway for a long moment before stepping into the life she never expected to be living.

Nothing looked the way she thought it would.

The path ahead was unfamiliar. The plans she once held had fallen apart in ways she had never prepared for. The chapter she was in now was not one she would have written for herself. If she had been given the choice, she would have chosen something gentler, something clearer, something far less painful.

But this was the chapter before her.

And she was trying, with trembling faith, to trust God in a story she never would have chosen.

Maybe you know that feeling.

Maybe you have found yourself living inside a chapter you never asked for, never imagined, and never would have picked if the pen had been in your hand.

There are chapters in life we would never have chosen for ourselves.

If it had been up to us, we would have skipped them.
We would have turned the page sooner.
We would have chosen joy instead of sorrow, peace instead of pain, healing instead of heartbreak, and clarity instead of confusion.

But life does not always unfold according to our choosing.

Sometimes the story takes a turn we never wanted.
Sometimes the path becomes harder than we imagined.
Sometimes we find ourselves walking through a chapter we never prayed for, never expected, and never would have picked.

These are the chapters that stretch the heart in painful ways.

The chapter of loss.
The chapter of waiting.
The chapter of betrayal.
The chapter of sickness.
The chapter of disappointment.
The chapter of unanswered questions.
The chapter of change you did not ask for.

And when you are living inside a chapter you did not choose, it is easy to wrestle with one aching question:

Lord, why did this have to be part of my story?

That is a tender question.

Because sometimes the pain is not only in what happened. Sometimes the pain is also in the fact that you never wanted it to happen at all. You would have chosen a different road. A different outcome. A gentler page.

And yet here you are.

Trying to trust God in a chapter you would never have written.

That kind of surrender is not easy. It is one thing to trust God when life is unfolding the way you hoped. It is another thing to trust Him when the story has turned in a direction you did not want.

But even when a chapter was not your choice, it is still not outside the hands of God.

That does not mean God delights in your pain.
It does not mean He is careless with your sorrow.
It does not mean every painful thing reflects His perfect desire.

But it does mean this:

Nothing enters your story beyond His ability to redeem.

He is still sovereign in the unexpected.
Still present in the unwanted.
Still faithful in the chapter you would never have written.

Isaiah 55:8–9 reminds us:

"For My thoughts are not your thoughts, neither are your ways My ways," saith the Lord. For as the heavens are higher than the earth, so are My ways higher than your ways and My thoughts than your thoughts."

There are things we do not understand.

There are chapters we wish could be erased.
There are moments we wish had never happened.
There are roads we would never have walked by choice.

Yet God, in His wisdom, knows how to meet us even there.

He knows how to bring His presence into unwanted places.
He knows how to speak peace into painful chapters.
He knows how to draw something holy from stories that felt unwanted and hard.

One of the clearest examples of this in Scripture is Joseph.

He would not have chosen betrayal by his brothers.
He would not have chosen the pit.
He would not have chosen slavery.
He would not have chosen prison.

Those were chapters he did not choose.

And yet, God was with him in every one of them.

What others meant for evil, God was able to use for good. Joseph could not see the full purpose while he was in the middle of the pain, but later he could say:

"But as for you, ye thought evil against me; but God meant it unto good…"
(Genesis 50:20)

What a powerful truth.

A chapter you did not choose may still become a chapter God uses.

Not because the pain itself was good.
Not because betrayal, sorrow, or suffering are holy in themselves.
But because God is so powerful, so wise, and so redemptive that He can work even through what you would never have chosen.

That gives hope to the grieving heart.

Because many of us are living with chapters we did not choose.

Some did not choose the wounds they carry.
Some did not choose the losses they mourn.
Some did not choose the burdens they bear.
Some did not choose the long road they now walk.

And yet, even here, God is still present.

He does not wait for the chapter to become pleasant before He enters it.
He does not say, "I will meet you only in the easy parts."
He comes into the hard places too.

He comes into the hospital room.
He comes into the lonely house.

He comes into the season of grief.
He comes into the chapter of heartbreak.
He comes into the life that feels unfamiliar after everything changed.

He comes near.

That is the mercy of God.

One woman once said that after her life changed in a way she never would
have chosen, the hardest part was not only the pain, but the feeling that she
had been taken off the road she thought she was supposed to be on. She
grieved not only what happened, but also what she thought would happen.
That is a very real kind of sorrow.

Sometimes we are mourning a loss.
Sometimes we are mourning a future we thought we would have.
Sometimes we are mourning the version of life we expected to be living
by now.

And that grief matters too.

Sometimes the chapter you did not choose becomes the place where you
learn God's nearness in ways you never knew before. Sometimes the
unwanted chapter becomes the place where your roots go deeper, your
prayers grow truer, and your dependence on Him becomes more real than
it has ever been.

We would not choose the pain.

But we can still choose to trust God in it.

That is the invitation.

You may not have chosen the chapter, but you can choose how you will
walk through it.

You can walk through it bitter, alone, and without surrender.
Or you can walk through it with tears, honesty, and faith, holding tightly
to the hand of the One who still writes with purpose.

Trusting God in an unwanted chapter does not mean pretending it does not
hurt.
It does not mean calling pain good.
It does not mean you cannot grieve what was lost.

It means bringing your real heart to Him and saying:

**"Lord, I would not have chosen this. But I still choose to trust You
here."**

That kind of trust is precious.

It is easy to trust God when life is unfolding the way you hoped.
It is deeper to trust Him when it is not.

Jesus Himself understood the weight of an unwanted cup. In the garden,
He prayed:

**"O my Father, if it be possible, let this cup pass from me: nevertheless
not as I will, but as thou wilt."**
(Matthew 26:39)

What holy surrender.

Jesus understood sorrow.
He understood anguish.
He understood costly obedience.
He understood what it meant to trust the Father in a painful chapter.

So, if you are living through a chapter you did not choose, you are not
alone in that place.

Your Savior understands.

He understands grief.
He understands the ache of surrender.
He understands what it feels like to carry a cup you did not want.

And He will walk with you through every page.

There is comfort in knowing that God is not only Lord of the chapters you enjoy. He is also Lord of the chapters that confuse you, wound you, and stretch your faith. He remains faithful even when the story takes a path you never would have written.

And though you may not understand this chapter now, that does not mean it is purposeless.

God may use it to deepen your compassion.
He may use it to strengthen your faith.
He may use it to loosen your grip on this world and draw your heart closer to heaven.
He may use it to prepare you to comfort someone else one day.
He may use it to reveal His nearness in ways you would not have known otherwise.

You may not see all of that now.

And you do not need to force meaning too quickly.

Sometimes the first step is simply to admit:

"This is not the chapter I would have chosen."

And then, gently, to say:

"But God, I trust You to meet me here."

That is enough for today.

One day, you may look back and see that the chapter you would never have chosen became a sacred place where God held you, carried you, taught you, and revealed His faithfulness in deeper ways than before.

Until then, be gentle with yourself.

You are allowed to grieve the chapter you did not want.
You are allowed to feel the ache of what was lost.
You are allowed to tell God the truth about how hard this page feels.

And you are also allowed to hope.

Because even the chapters you did not choose are still within the reach of God's redeeming hands.

He is still with you.
Still strengthening you.
Still carrying you.
Still writing.

And He knows how to bring purpose, mercy, and beauty even from the pages you never would have chosen for yourself.

Scripture for This Chapter

Genesis 50:20
"But as for you, ye thought evil against me; but God meant it unto good..."

Reflection

What chapter of your life did you never want or choose?
Can you honestly bring that pain to God and ask Him to meet you there with His presence, strength, and redeeming grace?

Prayer

Lord, there are chapters in my life I never would have chosen.
Some pages have brought pain, loss, and sorrow that I still do not fully
understand. But thank You that even the unwanted chapters are not outside
Your hands. Meet me in this place, strengthen me where I feel weak, and
help me trust that You can still bring purpose and beauty from what I
would never have written for myself. Teach me to surrender this chapter to
You and walk through it with faith.
In Jesus' name, amen.

Closing Line

**Even the chapters you did not choose are still held in the wise and
loving hands of God.**

Chapter 9

Grace for the Unfinished Places

Monica closed the journal on her lap and leaned back in her chair with a quiet sigh.

She had been writing down prayers, hopes, and the things she believed God was doing in her life. And as she looked back over older pages, she could see that some things had changed. There had been growth. There had been healing. There had been prayers God had answered in beautiful ways.

But there were still places that felt unfinished.

A few prayers were still waiting.
A few wounds were still tender.
A few questions still had no clear answer.
And a few parts of her heart still felt like works in progress.

She loved God. She was trying to trust Him. But if she was honest, there were moments when she felt discouraged that she was not further along by now.

Maybe you know that feeling too.

Maybe you look at your life and see evidence of God's faithfulness, but also places that still feel incomplete. Maybe you are grateful for how far He has brought you, yet still aware of the parts that are healing slowly, growing slowly, unfolding slowly.

There are places in life that still feel unfinished.

Prayers, still waiting for answers.
Healing, still in process.

Dreams, still not fully formed.
Questions still without explanation.
Wounds that are better than before, but not completely healed.

Unfinished places can be hard on the heart.

We often want things tied neatly together.
We want clarity.
We want closure.
We want peace without struggle.
We want the chapter to be complete and the story to make sense.

But much of life is lived in the unfinished.

We live between promise and fulfillment.
Between prayer and answer.
Between weakness and strength.
Between becoming and arrival.

And sometimes, it is in those unfinished places that we feel most aware of
our need.

We may feel frustrated that we are not further along.
We may feel discouraged that certain wounds still ache.
We may feel disappointed that some struggles still remain.
We may even feel ashamed that we are still growing in places we thought
would already be settled.

But God is full of grace for unfinished places.

He is not impatient with your process.
He is not ashamed of your weakness.
He is not frustrated that you are still healing, still learning, still becoming.

He knows you are not finished yet.

And He does not despise you for that.

Philippians 1:6 gives us such tender reassurance:

"Being confident of this very thing, that He who hath begun a good work in you will perform it until the Day of Jesus Christ."

What God begins, He continues.

That means your unfinished places do not surprise Him. The parts of your life still in process are not a disappointment to Him. The areas where you are still waiting, still healing, still learning to trust—all of it is fully known by Him.

He is still working.

Sometimes we show grace to others more easily than we show it to ourselves. We understand that others are growing. We understand that others are healing. We understand that others are learning through hard seasons. But when it comes to our own unfinished places, we often become harsh, impatient, and discouraged.

We say things like:

"I should be stronger by now."
"I should be over this by now."
"I should have more faith by now."
"I should not still struggle here."

But grace speaks differently.

Grace says:

God is still working in you.
God is still healing you.
God is still teaching you.
God is still carrying you.

Grace does not deny that there is more growth ahead.
It simply reminds you that you are loved while you are growing.

That matters deeply.

Because sometimes, the unfinished places are the very places where shame tries to speak the loudest. Shame says you are failing. Shame says you are not enough. Shame says that because the chapter is not complete, something must be wrong with you.

But shame is not the voice of God.

The voice of God calls you forward with truth and love.
He convicts, but He does not crush.
He leads, but He does not shame.
He corrects, but He does not condemn His children.

Romans 8:1 reminds us:

"There is therefore now no condemnation for those who are in Christ Jesus..."

No condemnation.

That means the unfinished places in your life are not places for condemnation. They are places where grace can meet you.

Grace for the heart still healing.
Grace for the prayer still waiting.
Grace for the dream still forming.
Grace for the soul still learning to trust.

One woman once shared that her hardest struggle was not the wound itself, but her disappointment with herself for still having the wound. She thought by now she would be stronger, steadier, less affected. But over time, God began to show her that healing is not measured by pretending the pain is gone. Healing is often measured by whether we keep bringing the pain to Him.

That is a freeing truth.

You do not have to be finished to be loved.
You do not have to be fully healed to be held by God.
You do not have to arrive before His grace can cover you.

God knows that deep work often takes time.

A flower does not bloom in one moment.
A tree does not grow strong in one day.
A wound does not always heal in a single breath.

Some of God's most beautiful work happens slowly.

Slowly, the heart softens.
Slowly, peace returns.
Slowly, faith grows deeper.
Slowly, wounds begin to close.
Slowly, strength rises again.

And in every slow step, grace is present.

In 2 Corinthians 12:9 says:

"And He said unto me, "My grace is sufficent for thee, for My strength is made perfect in weakness."

What a precious promise.

Not just grace for your strong days.
Grace for your weak days.
Not just grace for finished victories.
Grace for unfinished battles.
Not just grace for the places that shine.
Grace for the places still in process.

God's grace is sufficient.

Sufficient for the day you feel weary.
Sufficient for the day-old pain rises again.

Sufficient for the day you feel stuck in the middle.
Sufficient for the day you do not see much progress at all.

His grace does not run out because your process is taking time.

Sometimes we think the unfinished places make us less beautiful in God's
sight. But He often sees beauty where we only see incompleteness. He
sees the courage it takes to keep going. He sees the humility it takes to
keep depending on Him. He sees the faith it takes to keep trusting while
the work is still unfinished.

There is beauty in becoming.

There is beauty in a heart that still says yes to God while healing.
There is beauty in a soul that keeps praying while waiting.
There is beauty in a life that is still unfolding under His hand.

The unfinished places are not proof that God has abandoned the work.

They are often proof that He is still doing it.

A sculptor does not stop loving the piece because it is not finished yet. In
the same way, God does not stop loving you in the middle of the process.
He sees what He is shaping. He sees what you are becoming. He sees the
finished beauty even while you still feel unfinished.

That is why you can rest in His grace.

Not because everything is complete.
But because the One who is completing it is faithful.

If you still have questions, grace is there.
If you still carry some pain, grace is there.
If you still struggle in certain places, grace is there.
If you still feel unfinished, grace is there.

You do not have to hide your unfinished places from God.

Bring Him the part of you that still aches.
Bring Him the part that still fears.
Bring Him the part that still waits.
Bring Him the part that still feels incomplete.

He knows how to hold what is unfinished with tenderness.

And He knows how to keep writing with patience.

You may not be where you want to be yet.
You may not have all the answers yet.
You may not see the full picture yet.

But do not despise the place where grace is still meeting you.

The unfinished place may become the very place where you know the
gentleness of God more deeply than ever before. It may become the place
where you learn that your worth is not found in how finished you look, but
in whose hands, you are in.

And you are in His hands.

The hands of a faithful Father.
The hands of a patient Savior.
The hands of a God who does not leave His work half-done.

So be at peace in the process.

Let grace cover the places that still need time.
Let grace speak louder than shame.
Let grace remind you that God is not finished, and neither are you.

The unfinished places of your life are still under His care.
Still under His mercy.
Still under His hand.

And because of that, there is hope.

One day, you will see more clearly what He was doing all along. One day, the places that felt incomplete may become part of a testimony of grace. One day, you may look back and realize that even in the unfinished, God was holding you, shaping you, and loving you every step of the way.

Until then, receive His grace.

Grace for today.
Grace for the weakness.
Grace for the slow growth.
Grace for the unfinished places.

It is enough.

Scripture for This Chapter

2 Corinthians 12:9
"My grace is sufficient for thee: for My strength is made perfect in weakness."

Reflection

What unfinished place in your life have you been struggling to accept? Can you let God meet that place with grace instead of shame, and trust Him to continue the work He has begun?

Prayer

Lord, thank You for Your grace over every unfinished place in my life. Thank You that You are not impatient with me while I am still healing, growing, waiting, and becoming. Help me not to condemn myself for the

parts of my story still in process. Teach me to rest in Your sufficient grace and trust that You are still working in every area that feels incomplete. Cover my weakness with Your strength and my unfinished places with Your peace.
In Jesus' name, amen.

Closing Line

Where you still feel unfinished, God still pours out grace.

Chapter 10

Beauty from Ashes

Ruth stood in the middle of what was left and tried to imagine beauty again.

For a long time, she could not.

Too much had changed. Too much had been lost. The life she once knew felt far away now, like smoke after a fire. There were memories she still could not touch without feeling pain, and there were questions she still could not answer.

What remained felt like ashes.

Ashes of broken dreams.
Ashes of painful memories.
Ashes of loss, disappointment, betrayal, and grief.
Ashes of chapters that had burned through her heart and left her standing in a place she never thought she would be.

Maybe you understand that kind of place.

A place where something precious has been reduced to what feels like ruins. A place where you are no longer holding what once was, only what remains after sorrow has done its work.

Ashes are what remain after something has been consumed.

They remind us of what was lost.
They remind us of what once was.
They remind us of the fire we walked through and the things we could not keep from falling apart.

And when we look at the ashes of our lives, it can be hard to imagine beauty ever coming from them.

We may see only ruin.
We may see only pain.
We may see only the remains of what did not survive.

We may quietly ask:

Can anything good come from this?
Can anything beautiful rise from what has been broken?
Can God really make something new from all that has been lost?

And by His grace, the answer is yes.

God, is able to bring beauty from ashes.

Not because ashes are beautiful in themselves.
Not because pain is pleasant.
Not because loss is easy.

But because God is a Redeemer.

He is able to step into the places of ruin and begin creating again. He is able to breathe hope into what feels lifeless. He is able to bring healing where there has been heartbreak, peace where there has been torment, and purpose where there has been pain.

Isaiah 61:3 gives us this precious promise:

"To appoint unto them that mourn in Zion, to give unto them beauty for ashes, the oil of joy for mourning, the garment of praise for the spirit of heaviness, that they might be called trees of righteousness, the planting of the Lord, that He might be glorified"

What a tender exchange.

Beauty for ashes.
Joy for mourning.
Praise for heaviness.

This is the heart of God.

He does not only see the ashes. He knows what to do with them. He does not look at your broken places and turn away. He does not stand at the ruins of your pain and call the story finished.

He begins the work of redemption there.

Sometimes we want God to erase every hard thing completely. We want the ashes gone. We want the sorrow undone. We want the chapter rewritten as if the pain never happened. But God often does something deeper than erasing.

He redeems.

He takes what was meant to destroy and begins to weave grace through it. He takes what left you, mourning and begins to plant comfort in its place. He takes what felt ruined and begins to draw out beauty that could only come through His healing touch.

That is not something only God can explain.
It is something only God can do.

Ashes can come in many forms.

The ashes of a relationship that ended.
The ashes of trust that was broken.
The ashes of years that felt wasted.
The ashes of innocence damaged by painful experiences.
The ashes of a dream that did not survive the fire.

And when those ashes settle over the heart, it can feel like life will never bloom again.

One woman once said that after a devastating season, she did not know
how to pray for restoration because she could not even picture it anymore.
She believed God was good, but she could not imagine beauty rising from
what had already turned to ashes. Maybe you have felt that way too.
Sometimes grief makes it hard to imagine anything beyond survival.

But do not forget this: the same God who formed the earth from nothing is
still able to create beauty from what feels empty, ruined, and undone.

He is a God of resurrection.
He is a God of restoration.
He is a God who brings life where death once seemed to speak the loudest.

That means the ashes are not the final word.

Pain is not the final word.
Loss is not the final word.
Disappointment is not the final word.
The fire you walked through is not the final word.

God is.

And when God speaks over ashes, He speaks with redemptive power.

Sometimes beauty from ashes does not arrive all at once.

Sometimes it comes slowly.

Slowly, hope begins to rise again.
Slowly, peace returns to the heart.
Slowly, strength grows where weakness once lived.
Slowly, joy visits again in places that once knew only sorrow.

This kind of beauty is often gentle.

It does not rush the grieving heart.
It does not demand instant answers.
It does not pretend the fire did not hurt.

Instead, it reveals the faithfulness of God in the middle of what did hurt.

Beauty from ashes might look like:
peace after a long storm,
healing after deep wounds,
wisdom after painful chapters,
compassion born from suffering,
or a testimony that points others to the goodness of God.

Sometimes the beauty is not in getting back exactly what was lost.
Sometimes the beauty is in what God forms in you through the process—a deeper faith, a softer heart, a stronger trust, a more intimate walk with Him.

That kind of beauty is sacred.

It may not look like what you once imagined.
But it can still be beautiful in ways you could not have seen before.

Romans 8:28 reminds us that God works all things together for good to them that love Him. That does not mean every painful thing is good. It means God is able to work even through painful things for a greater good.

Only God can take ashes and bring forth something holy.

Only God can look at what has been burned down and say,
"I am not finished here."

He knows how to rebuild.
He knows how to restore.
He knows how to take the places that look ruined to human eyes and make them fruitful again.

If you are standing in ashes today, do not lose heart.

Do not assume the story is over.
Do not assume the fire destroyed every future hope.
Do not assume the broken chapter can never hold beauty again.

God is still able.

He may not bring beauty in the exact way you expected.
He may not restore things on your timetable.
He may not answer every question about why the fire came.

But He can still bring beauty.

Beauty that carries His fingerprints.
Beauty that comes through healing.
Beauty that comes through faith refined by fire.
Beauty that comes through surrender, grace, and the nearness of His presence.

Sometimes the beauty is simply this:

You survived by the mercy of God.

Sometimes the beauty is that your heart still prays.
Sometimes the beauty is that you still believe.
Sometimes the beauty is that though you have walked through the fire, you still know the Lord has held you every step of the way.

That is beautiful in His sight.

And sometimes, in time, the very ashes that once marked your sorrow become the ground where a testimony begins to grow. The pain that once made you weep becomes the place where others find hope through your story. The chapter that once looked ruined becomes the place where God's redeeming mercy shines the brightest.

This is why you must not despise the ashes.

Bring them to God.

Bring Him the remains of what was lost.
Bring Him the sorrow you still carry.

Bring Him the grief you cannot fully explain.
Bring Him the ruined places you do not know how to rebuild.

He knows what to do with ashes.

He knows how to take what looks empty and fill it with purpose.
He knows how to take what feels ruined and breathe life into it again.
He knows how to take mourning and slowly wrap it in comfort, grace, and beauty.

You may not see it all yet.
You may still feel surrounded by the remains of a painful chapter.
But do not mistake the presence of ashes for the absence of God.

He is there too.

He is in the place of rebuilding.
He is in the place of grieving.
He is in the place of slow healing.
He is in the place where beauty is still being born.

And because He is there, the ashes do not get the last word.

God does.

So let your heart hope again.

The God who promised beauty for ashes has not changed.
The God who restores has not changed.
The God who redeems broken stories has not changed.

He is still able to bring something beautiful from what hurts you.

And one day, you may look back and realize that the place you thought had become only ashes was also the place where God began one of the most beautiful works of His grace in your life.

Scripture for This Chapter

Isaiah 61:3

"To appoint unto them that mourn in Zion, to give unto them beauty for ashes, the oil of joy for mourning, the garment of praise for the spirit of heaviness, that they might be called trees of righteousness, the planting of the Lord, that He might be glorified."

Reflection

What ashes are you carrying in this season of your life?
Can you place those broken remains into God's hands and trust Him to bring beauty, healing, and purpose from them in His way and time?

Prayer

Lord, You see every ash-covered place in my life.
You see the sorrow, the loss, the broken dreams, and the painful remains of chapters I never wanted. Thank You that You are the God who gives beauty for ashes. Please take the places in me that feel ruined and breathe Your healing, hope, and redemption into them. Help me trust that even from what was lost, You are still able to bring something beautiful by Your grace.
In Jesus' name, amen.

Closing Line

The ashes may tell you what was lost, but God can still tell a beautiful story from what remains.

Chapter 11

The Author Has Not Left the Page

Elena sat by the window with her Bible open, but for a long while she did not read.

She was tired.

Not only tired in body, but tired in spirit. She had been praying. She had been waiting. She had been trying to stay faithful in a season that felt painfully quiet. She still believed in God. She still loved Him. But if she was honest, there were moments when she wondered why His presence felt harder to sense than before.

The chapter she was living in felt still.

No clear answer.
No visible change.
No dramatic breakthrough.
Just a long stretch of quiet days and a heart asking questions it did not know how to settle.

And in that silence, one thought kept rising:

Lord, are You still here?

Maybe you have known that feeling too.

Not that you stopped believing, but that you grew weary in the quiet. Not that you turned away from God, but that you longed for some clear reminder that He had not turned away from you. There are seasons when the soul aches, not only because life is hard, but because heaven feels so still.

There are times in life when God feels quiet.

You pray, but the heavens seem silent.
You wait, but no clear answer comes.
You look for signs of movement, but everything feels still.
And in that silence, the heart can begin to wonder if it has somehow been forgotten.

These are tender moments.

Because sometimes it is not only the pain of the chapter that weighs on us. It is the feeling that heaven has grown quiet in the middle of it. The soul longs for reassurance. It longs for something clear, something certain, something that says:

"I am with you, and I have not forgotten your story."

But when that reassurance does not come in the way we expected, it can feel lonely.

We may wonder if God has stepped back.
We may wonder if He is disappointed.
We may wonder if the silence means absence.

But silence is not the same as abandonment.

The Author has not left the page.

Just because God feels quiet does not mean He is gone.
Just because you cannot trace His hand does not mean He is no longer writing.
Just because the chapter feels still does not mean the story has been forgotten.

God is often at work in ways too deep for us to see in the moment.

He may be shaping things behind the scenes.
He may be preparing what is not yet ready.

He may be strengthening your heart in hidden ways.
He may be teaching you to trust His presence more than your feelings.

We often measure God's nearness by what we can feel. When peace comes easily, we say He is near. When answers come quickly, we say He is moving. When strength rises in our hearts, we say He is present.

But God's faithfulness is not measured by our emotions.

He is present because He is faithful.
He is near because He promised to be near.
He is still writing because He does not walk away from His children.

Hebrews 13:5 gives us this precious promise:

"I will never leave thee, nor forsake thee."

Never.

Not in the bright chapters.
Not in the dark ones.
Not in the chapters full of praise.
Not in the chapters full of tears.
Not in the seasons when you feel strong.
Not in the seasons when you feel barely able to hold on.

Never.

That word matters deeply when the soul feels alone.

Because there will be moments when God's presence feels less like a burning fire and more like a quiet holding. Less like thunder and more like a whisper. Less like sudden rescue and more like steady companionship through the valley.

But quiet presence is still presence.

Just because He does not shout does not mean He is absent.
Just because He does not answer every question immediately does not
mean He has stepped away.
Just because the page is painful does not mean the Author has stopped
writing.

One of the most beautiful examples of this is found in the book of Esther.

God's name is not mentioned directly there, and yet His hand is
everywhere. He is present in the timing, in the protection, in the courage,
in the turning of events. His voice is not loudly recorded on every page,
but His faithfulness is woven all through the story.

Sometimes your life may feel like that.

You may not hear the answer you hoped for.
You may not see the miracle yet.
You may not understand what God is doing.

And yet, He is still there in the hidden places.
Still arranging.
Still protecting.
Still sustaining.
Still writing.

One woman once shared that the hardest part of her waiting season was
not only the waiting itself, but the fear that nothing was happening. She
said, "I felt like I was praying into silence." But later, when the chapter
finally unfolded, she could see that God had been working in ways she
never could have known while she was in the middle of it.

That is often how hidden faithfulness works.

Sometimes the chapter feels quiet because God is teaching us deeper trust.

Anyone can trust when the path is bright and clear. But when the night is
long, when the heart is weary, and when no obvious answer appears, trust

becomes more precious. It becomes a choice rooted not in visible evidence, but in the unchanging character of God.

This is not easy faith.
But it is beautiful faith.

It is, the faith that says:

"Even if I do not hear You clearly right now, I still believe You are here."
"Even if I do not understand this page, I still believe You are writing."
"Even if the chapter feels quiet, I still believe You have not left me."

That kind of trust honors God.

Psalm 139 reminds us that there is nowhere we can go from His presence. Whether in the heights or the depths, whether in light or darkness, He is there. What a comfort to the heart that feels alone.

There is no page of your story where God is missing.

Not in the hospital room.
Not in the empty house.
Not in the grieving season.
Not in the waiting room.
Not in the chapter where you smile on the outside but ache on the inside.

He is there.

You may not always feel Him, but feelings are not the final truth.

His Word is.

And His Word says He will never leave you.

The enemy often tries to use silence to plant lies. He whispers that if God loved you, He would answer faster. He whispers that if God were near,

you would not feel this lonely. He whispers, that the quiet means you have
been forgotten.

But those whispers are not truth.

God's love is not proven only by visible answers.
His presence is not limited to what you can sense.
His faithfulness does not fail because the chapter is quiet.

Sometimes God's greatest work happens in hiddenness.

Roots grow in hidden places.
Seeds break open in hidden places.
Deep healing often begins in hidden places.

And in the same way, God may be doing holy work in your life that has
not yet become visible. The quiet chapter may still be full of His activity,
even if you cannot yet name it.

If you are in a quiet season, do not assume the pen has been laid down.

The Author has not left the page.

He is still writing with wisdom.
Still writing with mercy.
Still writing with purpose.
Still writing with love.

You may be in a paragraph you do not understand.
You may be in a chapter where little seems to move.
You may be in a place where all you can do is pray simple prayers and
trust day by day.

That is enough.

You do not need to force clarity before it comes.
You do not need to pretend the silence is easy.
You do not need to hide the ache of wanting God to speak more clearly.

Bring all of that honestly to Him.

Say,
"Lord, I miss hearing You."
"Father, I need reassurance."
"God, this chapter feels quiet but help me trust that You are still here."

He welcomes those prayers.

And often, even in the silence, He gives grace for the day. He gives enough strength to rise. Enough peace to endure. Enough mercy to keep going. Enough light for the next step.

That too is evidence of His presence.

Sometimes we are looking for dramatic answers while overlooking daily grace.

The breath in your lungs.
The strength to keep praying.
The Scripture that meets you at the right time.
The quiet comfort that keeps you from falling apart.
The unexpected kindness that reminds you that you are seen.

These are small but holy reminders:

The Author has not left the page.

He is still with you.

And one day, you may look back and see that the chapter you feared was empty was actually full of hidden faithfulness. You may realize that while you thought heaven was quiet, God was carrying you more closely than ever. You may discover that the silence did not mean abandonment. It meant that the Author was still writing in ways you could not yet see.

So do not lose heart in the quiet chapter.

Keep praying.
Keep opening His Word.
Keep trusting His promises.
Keep placing one foot in front of the other by faith.

Because the Author has not left the page.

He is still in the story.
Still in the chapter.
Still in the silence.
Still in the unseen work.
Still in the unfolding.

And because He is still there, hope remains.

Scripture for This Chapter

Hebrews 13:5
"I will never leave thee, nor forsake thee."

Reflection

Have you been walking through a quiet season where God feels distant?
Can you trust His promises even when you cannot clearly feel His
presence, and believe that He has not left your story?

Prayer

Lord, there are times when the chapter feels quiet and I wonder where You
are.
Thank You for reminding me that silence is not abandonment and that

You have not left the page of my life. Help me trust Your presence even when I do not feel it strongly. Strengthen my faith in the quiet seasons, open my eyes to Your daily grace, and remind me that You are still near, still faithful, and still writing my story with love and purpose.
In Jesus' name, amen.

Closing Line

The chapter may feel quiet, but the Author has not left the page.

Chapter 12

Your Next Chapter Begins with Faith

Hannah stood at the doorway of something new, and for a moment, she did not move.

It was not that she did not want to go forward.
It was that going forward felt tender.

Too much had happened behind her. Too many prayers, too many tears, too many chapters that had stretched her heart in ways she never expected. She had learned to trust God in sorrow, in waiting, in unanswered questions, and in the ache of unfinished places. But now a new chapter was beginning to open, and instead of feeling only excitement, she felt something else too:

Uncertainty.

Because new beginnings can feel beautiful, but they can also feel fragile. They ask something of us. They ask us to step forward before we know exactly how the story will unfold.

Maybe you know that feeling.

Maybe God is opening a new chapter before you, and you want to trust Him, but part of your heart still trembles. Maybe you are standing between what has been and what is ahead, trying to believe that you can walk forward again.

Every story has moments of turning.

A page closes.
A new one begins.

A season ends.
Another season waits just ahead.

Sometimes we recognize these turning points clearly. Sometimes they come quietly, almost without warning. But whether they arrive with joy, uncertainty, or trembling, new chapters always ask something of us.

They ask us to move forward.

And moving forward is not always easy.

Sometimes we want to stay where things feel familiar, even if the chapter has been painful. Sometimes the known sorrow feels less frightening than the unknown future. Sometimes the heart hesitates because it has been hurt before, disappointed before, or left weary by what it has already carried.

So, when the next chapter begins to open, the soul may ask:

Can I trust again?
Can I hope again?
Can I walk forward when I do not know what the next page holds?

And the answer is yes—not because you know everything ahead, but because God goes with you.

Your next chapter begins with faith.

Not with full understanding.
Not with complete certainty.
Not with every question answered.

But with faith.

Faith is what takes the next step when the whole road is not yet visible.
Faith is what says yes to God before all the details are clear.
Faith is what opens trembling hands and says,
"Lord, I will trust You with what comes next."

That is a holy beginning.

We often think we need strength first, confidence first, answers first, and peace first. But many times, peace comes after the step of faith, not before it. Strength grows as we walk. Clarity unfolds as we obey. Courage rises as we trust.

Faith does not always feel bold.

Sometimes faith feels small, quiet, and trembling.

Sometimes faith sounds like:

"Lord, I am afraid, but I will go."
"Father, I do not know what is ahead, but I will follow."
"God, I still carry some wounds, but I believe You are leading me."

That is still faith.

And God honors it.

Hebrews 11:1 says:

"Now faith is the substance of things hoped for, the evidence of things not seen."

Faith lives in hope.
It trusts beyond what is visible.
It believes that what cannot yet be seen is still held in the hands of God.

This is how new chapters begin.

Not by controlling the future, but by trusting the Author.
Not by seeing the whole story at once, but by taking the next step in obedience.
Not by waiting until fear is gone, but by choosing trust in the middle of uncertainty.

Many people in Scripture stepped into new chapters this way.

Abraham left his country by faith, not knowing where he was going.
Moses stood before impossible waters by faith.
Ruth walked into an unknown future by faith.
Joshua crossed into promise by faith.
And the woman with the issue of blood reached for Jesus by faith.

Again and again, Scripture shows us that God meets those who step forward trusting Him.

He does not demand that you know everything first.
He asks for your heart, your trust, and your willingness to follow.

That means your next chapter does not have to begin with perfection.

It begins with surrender.

You may still have questions.
You may still have scars.
You may still feel unsure in certain ways.

But you can still move forward with God.

Because faith is not the absence of weakness.
It is the decision to place your weakness in His strength.

It is the choice to believe that the same God who carried you through the last chapter will also carry you through the next one. It is the quiet confidence that says:

"He has been faithful, and He will be faithful again."

That matters when the future feels unknown.

The truth is, none of us can fully see the next chapter before we live it. We do not know every joy, every trial, every lesson, or every blessing that may come. But we do know this:

God will already be there.

Before you arrive at the next page, He is already in it.
Before you step into the new chapter, He is already preparing grace for it.
Before the next need arises, He already knows how He will provide.
Before the next burden comes, He already knows how He will strengthen you.

What a comfort.

You are not walking into the future alone.
You are walking into a chapter already held in God's hands.

Isaiah 43:19 says:

"Behold, I will do a new thing; now it shall spring forth; shall ye not know it? I will even make a way in the wilderness and rivers in the desert."

God is not only the Lord of what has been.
He is also the Lord of what is ahead.

He still writes new beginnings.
He still opens new doors.
He still restores hope.
He still calls weary hearts forward into fresh mercies.

One woman once shared that after a long season of heartbreak, she was almost more afraid of hope than of pain. Pain had become familiar. Hope felt risky. She said that taking one small step into a new beginning felt harder than surviving some of the earlier chapters. But that is often how healing works. Sometimes moving forward is tender because it asks us to trust again.

And yet, that is exactly where faith begins to shine.

Sometimes the next chapter begins after great pain. Sometimes it begins after waiting, after heartbreak, after loss, or after a long season of uncertainty. And because of that, new beginnings can feel delicate. They can feel fragile. They can feel difficult to trust.

That is why your next chapter begins not with pressure, but with faith.

Not pressure to have it all together.
Not pressure to never feel afraid.
Not pressure to understand every turn of the road.

But faith that God will meet you as you go.

If the last chapter wounded you, faith says healing can still continue.
If the last chapter disappointed you, faith says hope can still rise again.
If the last chapter left you waiting, faith says God still has purpose ahead.
If the last chapter felt unfinished, faith says God is still writing.

The new chapter may not look like what you expected.

But it can still be full of God.

And that is enough.

You do not need to force tomorrow open.
You do not need to rush the page turning.
You do not need to invent your own ending.

You simply need to walk with the Author.

Step by step.
Prayer by prayer.
Choice by choice.
Faith by faith.

That is how beautiful new chapters begin.

They begin when a heart says yes to God again.
They begin when a weary soul dares to hope again.

They begin when a wounded spirit chooses trust again.
They begin when trembling hands still reach for the hand of the Lord.

So, if a new chapter is opening before you, do not be afraid.

You may not know all that it will hold.
But you know the One who holds it.

And that changes everything.

The same God who was with you in your tears will be with you in your new beginning.
The same God who sustained you in the waiting will sustain you in the walking.
The same God who comforted you in the broken places will strengthen you in the next place.

He has not brought you this far to leave you now.

Philippians 3:13–14 reminds us to forget those things which are behind and reach forth unto those things which are before, pressing toward the mark. This does not mean pretending the past never happened. It means refusing to stay imprisoned by old chapters when God is calling you forward.

There is grace for the past.
There is healing for the wounds.
There is hope for what lies ahead.

So, lift your eyes.

The next chapter begins with faith.
Not fear.
Not shame.
Not despair.

Faith.

Faith to believe that God is still good.
Faith to believe that He is still leading.
Faith to believe that what is ahead is still under His care.
Faith to believe that your story is still unfolding under the hand of a loving
Father.

And one day, you may look back and see that the chapter you were once
afraid to enter became a place of growth, grace, strength, and quiet
miracles you could not have imagined before.

So, take the step.

Even if it is small.
Even if it is trembling.
Even if it is only enough for today.

Take it with God.

Because your next chapter does not begin with all the answers.

It begins with faith.

Scripture for This Chapter

Hebrews 11:1
*"Now faith is the substance of things hoped for, the evidence of things not
seen."*

Reflection

What next chapter is God inviting you to step into?
What would it look like for you to begin that chapter with faith, even if
you do not yet know every detail?

Prayer

Lord, thank You that every next chapter of my life is already in Your hands.
When I feel uncertain about what lies ahead, help me begin with faith.
Teach me to trust You even when I do not see the whole road and give me courage to take the next step in obedience. Heal any fear that holds me back, strengthen my heart for what is ahead, and remind me that You will go with me into every new page You write.
In Jesus' name, amen.

Closing Line

You do not need to know the whole story to begin the next chapter—you only need faith in the Author.

Conclusion

The Story Is Still in His Hands

There comes a moment at the end of a book when the reader pauses before closing the final page.

Not because the story is forgotten, but because it lingers.

The words remain.
The truth settles deeper.
The heart carries something forward.

That is my prayer for you now.

As you come to the end of this book, I pray that one truth rests deeply in your heart:

God is still writing your story.

He is still writing through the tears.
He is still writing through the waiting.
He is still writing through the healing.
He is still writing through the chapters you did not choose.
He is still writing through the quiet places, the unfinished places, and the pages you do not yet understand.

You may not know exactly what the next chapter holds.

You may still have questions.
You may still carry some pain.
You may still be waiting for prayers to be answered and promises to unfold.

But even here, your life is still in His hands.

And there is no safer place for your story to be.

The world may tell you that a broken chapter means a broken future. Fear may whisper that the pain has the final word. Discouragement may try to convince you that the silence means nothing is happening.

But God says otherwise.

He is the Redeemer of broken stories.
He is the Healer of wounded hearts.
He is the Restorer of what has been lost.
And He is the faithful Author who never abandons His work.

He sees every page.
He knows every tear.
He understands every silence.
And He holds every tomorrow.

That means you do not have to be afraid of the unfinished places.

You do not have to lose heart in the waiting.
You do not have to give up in the middle.
You do not have to believe that the ashes are the end.

The God who began this story with purpose is still carrying it forward with grace.

One day, you may look back and see more clearly what you cannot fully see now. One day, you may realize that the chapters you feared most were also the places where God held you most closely. You may see that the waiting was not wasted, the tears were not forgotten, and the broken places were not beyond His healing touch.

Until that day, keep walking by faith.

Keep praying.
Keep trusting.

Keep surrendering.
Keep hoping.

Not because every chapter is easy, but because the Author is faithful.

One woman once said that the greatest comfort she found was not in knowing how her story would turn out, but in knowing whose hands it was in. That is where peace begins for all of us too. Not in certainty about every outcome, but in trust in the One who holds every outcome.

You do not have to carry the whole story alone.

You do not have to understand every page before you trust Him.
You do not have to know the ending before you place your hand in His.

Your story is still in His hands.

And because it is in His hands, there is still hope.

So step into the next chapter with faith.

Step into it with prayer.
Step into it with trust.
Step into it knowing that the same God who has carried you this far will carry you still.

The story is not over.
The Author is still writing.
And in His hands, every page can still become a testimony of grace.

So, if the road ahead still feels tender, take heart.

If the future still holds unanswered questions, take heart.
If the page still feels unfinished, take heart.
If your hands still tremble a little as you turn toward what comes next, take heart.

You are not turning the page alone.

The Author goes with you.

And He is faithful to finish what He has begun.

Closing Scripture

Jeremiah 29:11
"For I know the thoughts that I think toward you, saith the Lord, thoughts of peace, and not of evil, to give you an expected end."

Final Closing Line

The page may be unfinished, but the Author is faithful—and your story is still in His hands.

About the Author

About the Author

Dr. Lende Click is a Christian author, speaker, counselor, and founder of **Lende Click Publishing**. She writes faith-filled books that encourage women, children, and families to grow in courage, healing, identity, and trust in God.

Born and raised in Cebu, Philippines, Dr. Click's life has been marked by trials, grace, healing, and redemption. Through many fires, she has seen the faithfulness of God again and again. Her testimony and ministry are rooted in the belief that the Lord brings beauty from ashes, strength from suffering, and purpose from pain.

Through her writing, Dr. Click seeks to encourage hearts, strengthen faith, and remind readers that God is present even in life's hardest seasons. She is the author of several inspirational Christian books, Bible studies, devotionals, children's books, and faith-based stories, including works from the **Faith & Courage** collection and books for women seeking spiritual growth, healing, and restoration.

In addition to writing, Dr. Click serves as a Christian counselor. She is an **NCCA Licensed Professional Clinical Counselor, Certified Temperament Counselor, NCCA Licensed Clinical Pastoral Counselor**, and **NCCA Licensed Christian Counselor**. She is also advanced certified in **Death and Grief Therapy** and **Integrated Marriage and Family Therapy**, and she is a member of the **American Association of Christian Counselors (AACC)** and the **National Christian Counselors Association (NCCA)**.

Dr. Click writes with a special heart for women who are hurting, children in need, and those who long to know God more deeply. Through her books and ministry, she desires to point every reader to Jesus Christ—the

One who saves, restores, carries, and never leaves His children alone in the fire.

Some proceeds from her work help support children in Cebu, Philippines. She currently lives in Augusta, Georgia, and continues to write books that inspire faith, courage, healing, and hope.

Lende Click Publishing
Inspiring hearts through faith and stories.

Other Books by Lende Click

Faith & Courage Children's Books

Sammy the Shy Snail's Big Race
A gentle story of courage, faith, and believing God can help you do hard things.

Bella the Brave Butterfly and the Stormy Day
A sweet story teaching children courage and trust in God during fearful times.

Toby the Turtle Who Trusted God
A faith-filled story about learning to trust God one step at a time.

Delen's Story: Faith Like Sunshine
An uplifting story of faith, hope, and God's light shining through every season.

Inspirational & Devotional

The Gift of Godly Friendship
A Bible study for women who long for meaningful, godly connection.

Daughters of the King
An 8-week Bible study workbook for women growing in faith, identity, and purpose.

Prayers of a Daughter of the King
A devotional journey of prayer, strength, and deeper intimacy with God.

When God Carries a Woman Through the Fire
A powerful encouragement for women walking through pain, testing, and restoration.

A Life Redeemed
A story of God's grace, healing, and redeeming love.

Serving the Lord with a Willing Heart
A 12-Week Bible Study on Faithful Service for the Lord

Healing for the Woman Who Has Been Hurt
A Bible Study for Finding Hope, Restoration, and Wholeness in Christ

Christian Fantasy

The Kingdom of Everlight
An epic faith-filled fantasy story of courage, destiny, and the triumph of light over darkness.

Book One in The Kingdom of Everlight Series

The Kingdom of Everlight: The Crown of Hidden Fire

An Epic Christian Fantasy of Courage, Sacrifice, and the Light That Darkness Cannot Destroy

Book Two in The Kingdom of Everlight Series